'D CHEW YEW!

A collection of creatures by LISA JONES
and rhymes by JOANNA SKIPWITH

A companion for I CHOOSE YOU!

SILVER JUNGLE

A worm will chew
Enough to wriggle through,
Then he'll wriggle through enough
To chew some more.
And sometimes, as he wiggles through,
Forgetting where he's wriggling to,
He stops to have a giggle
At the core.

This crocodile with his charming smile
Looks far too sweet to me.
Remember that he likes to eat...

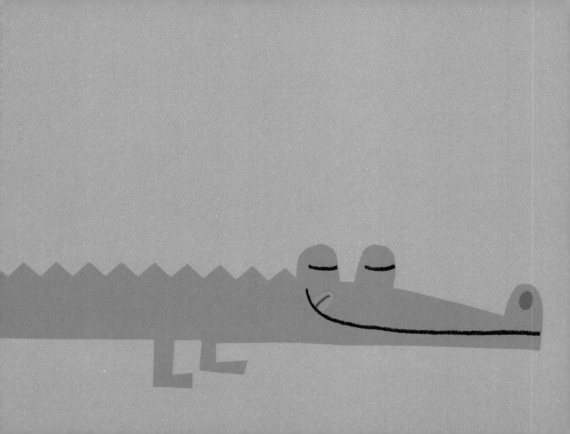

...young children for his tea.

Recycling is a good idea,
And very good for foxes.
We love the bits of chicken
That you leave behind in boxes.

The man in the pet shop said:
'We don't stock caterpillars.
They're small and not much fun.'
But surely he should market me...

...as 'Two for the price of one!'

I'm not a vampire, I promise.
I eat ripe figs and bananas.
If you're feeling brave
Then come to my cave.
Meet me at 8
In pyjamas.

On the northern rim
In the Arctic sea
Where ice floes brim with seals,
A polar bear
With snow-white hair
Dreams of frozen meals.

Swimming: Excellent
Fishing: Good
Rock-Hopping: Fair
Diving: Improving
Flying: Poor
Waddling: Shows natural flair

My trunk is a snorkel,
A trumpet, a nose
And a shower attachment
With flexible hose!

Is it safe to come out, skip about,
Run among the limpits and shout:
'I'm naked, I'm naked, look at me!'
Or should I show some modesty?

Today I saw, to my amazement,
A sausage jog along the pavement.
It scampered past on tiny feet,
Then turned the corner of the street,
Or was it...

...a Sausage Dog?

'Here little kitty',
The young girl said
As she reached
Through my bars
At the zoo.
I know it's a pity
To eat someone pretty...

...but what is a tiger to do?

This ladybird
Is very tiny,
Timid and tickly,
Crimson and shiny.
She sits on my hand
While I count her spots,
Which isn't so hard
As she hasn't got lots.

I'm a top performer,
The star of the show,
And I *must* have carrots
Wherever I go.

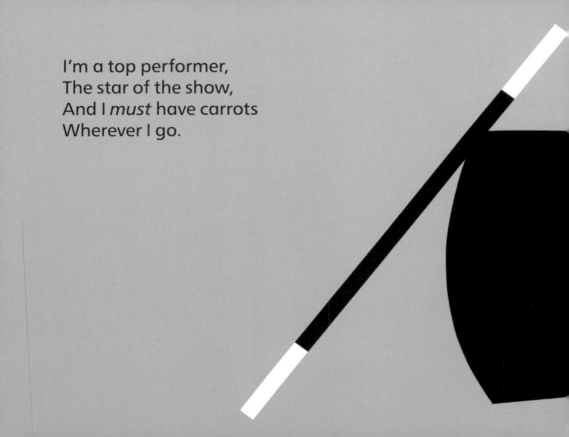

A beaver would chew
Anything wooden
Anything wooden would do.
Larch or pine,
Beech would be fine,
Even a bench or two.
A small canoe?
He could manage a few.
And private jetty?
Sure, straight through.
He'd even chew
On poisonous yew.
Anything wooden would do.

Did you know that beavers once roamed Britain, or at least beavered happily along its river banks, building dams and creating swimming pools for water voles and other wildlife? By the 18th century, however, they had been hunted to extinction, prized more for their fur and the oil secreted from their glands than for their land management.

Small groups of European beavers are now being reintroduced to Britain to see how they get on... Will there be an outbreak of gnawing? If you are a little concerned, please add a tree to our 'silver jungle'. It will be planted in the Caledonian forest in Scotland.

www.treesforlife.org/groves/silverjungle.html

www.silverjungle.com

Published by Silver Jungle Ltd
P.O. Box 51793, London NW1W 9AZ
www.silverjungle.com

Designed by Lisa Jones Studio
www.lisajonesstudio.com
Printed in England by Connekt Colour
on Splendorgel.

ISBN 978-0-9552652-4-2

Mixed Sources
Product group from well-managed
forests and other controlled sources
www.fsc.org   Cert no. TT-COC-002679
© 1996 Forest Stewardship Council

FSC